DC COMICS™

BATMAN™
SCIENCE

THE REAL-WORLD SCIENCE BEHIND BATMAN'S GEAR

BY AGNIESZKA BISKUP
AND TAMMY ENZ

BATMAN CREATED
BY BOB KANE

capstone
young readers

Published by Capstone Young Readers
A Capstone Imprint
1710 Roe Crest Drive
North Mankato, Minnesota 56003
www.capstonepub.com

STAR31641

Library of Congress Cataloging-in-Publication Data
Enz, Tammy.
  Batman science : the real-world science behind Batman's gear / by Tammy Enz and Agnieszka Biskup; Batman created by Bob Kane.
    pages cm
  Includes bibliographical references and index.
  Summary: "Explores the real-world science and engineering connections to the features of Batman's Batsuit, Utility Belt, road vehicles, and aircraft"—Provided by publisher.
  ISBN 978-1-62370-064-5 (paperback)   978-1-62370-674-6 (paperback, special order)
1. Technology—Juvenile literature. 2. Inventions—Juvenile literature. 3. Crime prevention—Technological innovations—Juvenile literature. 4. Batman (Fictitious character)—Juvenile literature. 5. Batman (Comic strip)—Juvenile literature. I. Biskup, Agnieszka. II. Title.
T48.E545 2014
600—dc23   2013028330

Editorial Credits
Christopher L. Harbo, editor; Veronica Scott, designer; Kathy McColley, production specialist

Photo Credits
Alamy: A. T. Willett, 89, Bob Daemmrich Photography/Marjorie Kamys Cotera, 54, Jeff Mood, 15 (bottom), louise murray, 72, motorlife, 83 (top), National Geographic Image Collection/Gregory A. Harlin, 50, WaterFrame, 73, ZUMA Press/Nancy Kaszerman, 93; AP Images: Mel Evans, 81 (b), Central Intelligence Agency, 131; Courtesy of Boston Dynamics, 95 (b); DARPA, 86; DoD photo by Luis Viegas, 60, MCSN Martin Carey, U.S. Navy, 60, Staff Sgt. Stephen Schester, U.S. Air Force, 17; Dreamstime: Editor77, 85, Lawrence Weslowski Jr, 29 (t), Sergei Bachlakov, 14; Getty Images: AFP/Kazuhiro Nogi, 45, Bloomberg, 103, Denver Post/Ernie Leyba, 31 (b), Time Life Pictures/Joseph Scherschel, 130, Time Life Pictures/Library of Congress, 135 (b); Glow Images: Science Faction/SuperStock, 20 (left), SuperStock/Science Faction, 53; LaserMotive, Inc., 123 (b); Library of Congress, 110; Louisiana Army and Air National Guard photo by 1st Lt. Angela Fry, 62; NASA, 9 (b), 83 (b), Dryden Flight Research Center/Steve Lighthill, 113 (b), Jim Ross, 135 (t); Newscom: AFP/Getty Images/Karen Bleier, 101, AFP/Getty Images/Toshifumi Kitamura, 81 (t), akg-images, 140, Araldo di Crollalanza, 116, Cal Sport Media/Paul Herbert, 95 (t), Europics, 117, Getty Images/AFP/Toshifumi Kitamura, 81 (t), imago sportfotodienst, 57, picture-alliance/dpa/Boris Roessler, 104, Reuters/Morris Mac Matzen, 111 (b), UPI/Kevin Dietsch, 70 (right), WENN.com, 99 (b), ZUMA Press/ChinaFotoPress, 38, ZUMA Press/Daily Mail/David Crump, 39, ZUMA Press/Sutton Motorsports, 79 (t), ZUMA Press/UPPA, 78-79; Science Source: GIPhotoStock, 32; Shutterstock: 501room, 18 (r), Alexandra Lande, 37, Andrey_Kuzmin, 71, 70 (l), ArtTomCat, 25, Carolina K. Smith MD, 20 (r), Christopher Parypa, 113 (top), digitalreflections, 51 (b), Distrikt 3, 22, Eugene Chernetsov, 76, farres, 44 (both), Fotokostic, 18 (l), Gavran333, 43, Greg Epperson, 48, Jason and Bonnie Grower, 87, Joe White, 56, Melissa Brandes, 46, Mi.Ti., 16, MO_SES, 111 (top), Olga Gabay, 141, PerseoMedusa, 125 (b), PinkBlue, 61, Sergio Schnitzler, 51 (t), TFoxFoto, 15 (t), Tooykrub, 59, Vitalii Nesterchuk, 49, ZRyzner, 29 (b); U.S. Air Force photo, 120, 128, Master Sgt. Jeremy Lock, 84, Senior Airman Felicia Juenke, 21, Staff Sgt. Brian Ferguson, 136, Staff Sgt. Joseph Swafford Jr., 92, Staff Sgt. Stacy L. Pearsall, 10, Tech. Sgt. Jeremy T. Lock, 65, Staff Sgt. Bennie J. Davis III, 88; U.S. Army photo by George Kenneth Lucey Jr. and Benson King, 125 (t), Kaye Richey, 11 (t), Markus Rauchenberger, 47 (t), Melvin G. Tarpley, 11 (b), Sgt. Pablo N. Piedra, 47 (b), Spc. Kayla Benson, 96, Spc. Kelly McDowell, 67, Spc. Ryan A. Cleary, 105, Staff Sgt. David Chapman, 63; U.S. Marine Corps photo by Cpl. David Hernandez, 68, Cpl. Garry J. Welch, 121, Cpl. Justin M. Boling, 123 (t), Lcpl Joey Chavez, 107; U.S. Navy photo, 119 (b), 77 (b), John Narewski, 69, Lt. Troy Wilcox, 34, MC2 Brian Morales, 119 (t), MC2 Julio Rivera, 139, MC2 Michael Lindsey, 23, MC2 Tony D. Curtis, 33, MC3 Billy Ho, 35, MC3 Mark El-Rayes, 114, MCSN Jonathan L. Correa, 13, MCSN Timothy A. Hazel, 127, PH2 John L. Beeman, 9 (t), PH3 Joshua Karsten, 126, PH3 Tucker M. Yates, 27, PO2 Robert J. Whelan, 106; U.S. Secert Service, 97; Wikimedia: Arpingstone, 129, Carla Cioffi, 133 (b), IFCAR, 77 (t), J. Glover, Atlanta, Georgia, 31 (t); Wikipedia: Bernd.Brincken, 115, BMK, 99 (t), Gryffinder, 112, J Clear, 133 (t), ravas51, 91

Design Elements: Shutterstock: BiterBig, ClickHere, Jason Winter

Printed in China.
042015   PO8916

TABLE OF CONTENTS

SUPER HERO SCIENCE AND ENGINEERING

Super heroes have battled crime in comic books and on the big screen for decades. While many of these heroes have amazing strength and incredible powers, Batman is a little different. He's not an alien from another planet. He doesn't wear magic rings or see through walls with X-ray vision. Under his suit and cape, the Dark Knight is a regular human being. He's Bruce Wayne of Gotham City.

But what Bruce lacks in superpowers, he easily makes up for with brains and brawn. As Batman, he relies on science and engineering to gain an advantage over his enemies. With his state-of-the-art suit, belt, and vehicles, Batman takes on Gotham City's criminal underworld with dazzling technology. From Batarangs to Batmobiles, the Caped Crusader stands ready for anything.

With all of this stunning technology, questions remain. Do Batman's gadgets and vehicles have any connection to the real world? Do grapnel guns, body armor, and rocket-boosted cars really exist? You bet—and the real-world connections stretch further than you've ever imagined. From wingsuits to stealth fighter jets to police duty belts, real-life connections abound. Batman may fight evil in a fictional world, but much of his gear is rooted in reality. Need proof? Get ready to see the real-world science and engineering behind the Dark Knight.

FACT:

BATMAN MADE HIS FIRST APPEARANCE IN *DETECTIVE COMICS* #27 IN 1939.

BATSUITS AND CAPES

THE SCIENCE BEHIND BATMAN'S BODY ARMOR

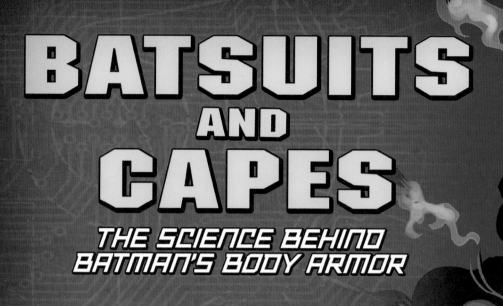

SECTION 1

To fight crime on the mean streets of Gotham City, you need body armor. For Batman, the layers and pieces of his Batsuit are the key to staying safe. His skintight suit may look thin, but it offers more protection than meets the eye.

DRESSING IN LAYERS

Staying warm and dry is as important in our world as it is in Batman's. Have you ever been told to wear lots of layers to stay warm? That's because multiple layers trap warm air in between them.

When it comes to bodysuits like Batman's, layers are important as well. For instance, divers wear snug, flexible wetsuits to keep warm in cold water. Wetsuits are also made of multiple layers. Some even have a thin metal lining to help reflect body heat. But most important, wetsuits have a layer of synthetic rubber called neoprene.

Neoprene is loaded with tiny nitrogen gas bubbles. The bubbles help stop heat from leaving your body, making neoprene a good insulator. Neoprene is also physically tough. It resists tearing from flexing and twisting. Neoprene is a great material to use if you move like a super hero.

A Navy diver wears a neoprene wetsuit to stay warm in the water.

SUITED FOR SPACE

Layered bodysuits offer protection all over our world—and even beyond. Astronauts gear up in amazing suits to survive in outer space. On spacewalks in sunlight, their suits shield them from temperatures hotter than boiling water. In the darkness their suits withstand temperatures that can drop to minus 250 degrees Fahrenheit (minus 157 degrees Celsius). Brrrr!

HIDING IN THE SHADOWS

As Batman keeps an eye on Gotham City's criminals, he doesn't want to be seen himself. It's no accident that his Batsuit uses mostly black and blue colors. The dark colors help him blend into the shadows.

In the real world, people use camouflage to avoid being seen. Camouflage, or camo, is coloring or covering that makes people, animals, or objects look like their surroundings. Soldiers wear different types of camo depending on where they are working. Most camo uses colors and patterns to hide something or someone.

A soldier wears green and gray camo to blend into her surroundings.

While camo can be a single color, patterns of different colored patches work best. This mottled pattern is called disruptive coloration. A soldier wearing green patterned camo in a jungle gives the brain a puzzle. Instead of seeing a soldier, the brain wants to connect the pattern's lines with the lines of the trees, leaves, and shadows. In this way, disruptive coloration helps disguise the shape of a person's body. A person wearing this type of camo appears to blend in with the surroundings.

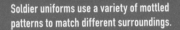

Soldier uniforms use a variety of mottled patterns to match different surroundings.

PICKING COLORS

When it comes to color, camo is all about matching the environment. To hide in forests, soldiers wear green and brown to match the leaves, ground, and tree bark. For snowy areas, their camo uses a mixture of white and gray. The camo soldiers wear in deserts is sometimes called chocolate-chip camouflage. Its mixture of brown and tan looks similar to chocolate-chip cookies.

INTO THE FIRE

Batman's enemies know how to turn up the heat on the Caped Crusader. Luckily the materials in the Batsuit can survive fires and fiery explosions. Do these kinds of materials exist in the real world?

Ever since people started using fire, they've looked for ways to avoid being burned. For centuries, natural materials such as wool offered some fire protection. But more recently scientists started making breakthroughs. In the 1960s they created a heat- and flame-resistant material called Nomex.

Nomex is made of ringlike molecules bonded together into tough, long chains. These chains create really strong fibers. Although Nomex burns when you hold it to a flame, it stops burning as soon as the flame is removed.

Just as important, Nomex fibers are poor conductors of heat. When fire touches Nomex, the woven fibers thicken and swell. This swelling creates a protective barrier between the heat source and the skin. The thickened fibers also prevent the material from melting or igniting. And it takes time for heat to travel through Nomex. Hopefully in those extra seconds, you've managed to put the fire out!

Firefighters on a U.S. Navy ship wear Nomex hoods to protect their heads and faces from fire.

FACT:

YOU MAY NOT REALIZE IT, BUT YOU PROBABLY HAVE NOMEX IN YOUR HOUSE. IT'S USED IN MANY OVEN GLOVES.

GOT NOMEX?

Nomex is so good at resisting heat and flame, it has become a go-to material for jobs where fire can be a hazard. Welders and glassblowers use gloves made of Nomex to protect their hands. Race car drivers wear suits with Nomex material to protect them from fiery crashes. Military pilots and aircrew wear flight suits made of Nomex. These suits protect them from cockpit fires. Even astronauts wear articles made of Nomex.

Race car driver Ryan Hunter-Reay wears a Nomex hood to protect his head from fire in the event of a crash.

But firefighters need Nomex most of all. They wear fire suits sometimes known as turnout gear or bunker gear. These suits have several protective layers made of heat- and fire-resistant materials, including Nomex. They protect from heat and burns, but also allow airflow. This airflow prevents moisture build-up within the suit itself. Firefighters typically wear Nomex hoods under their helmets to protect the ears, neck, and part of the face.

Nomex in a firefighter's turnout gear protects against the intense heat of a raging fire.

YOU'RE FIRED!

Normally, you want to avoid being set on fire. But not if you're a Hollywood stuntperson! We've all seen characters in movies go up in flames. These stunts are very dangerous. Stuntpeople wear Nomex suits under their characters' clothes and a special barrier gel to protect their skin. A full body burn may last 20 seconds. When the scene is done, the stuntperson falls face down. The fire is immediately put out with fire extinguishers.

BODY ARMOR

To fight crime, Batman puts himself in the line of fire. The Batsuit is the only thing that stands between him and all kinds of lethal impacts. To protect him, it includes body armor—a technology that has come a long way over the centuries.

The history of body armor spans thousands of years. Ancient tribes used animal hides and woven plant material for protection from cuts and scrapes. The ancient Romans covered their chests with metal breastplates. Full-body metal armor came into its glory by the 1400s. Medieval knights covered themselves from head to toe in metal plates to protect against sword thrusts or arrows.

Once cannons and guns were developed, traditional armor fell by the wayside. To protect from these kinds of impacts, metal armor would be too thick and heavy to wear.

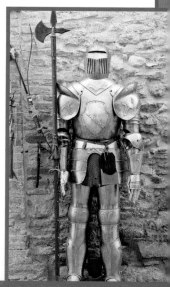

Medieval knights protected themselves with heavy metal armor.

Soldiers put on armored bomb suits before disabling explosive devices.

But as weapons have changed, body armor has evolved too. Today soldiers and police protect themselves with either hard or soft body armor. Hard body armor is similar to the metal armor of the Middle Ages. It protects well, but is heavy and cumbersome.

Soft body armor is woven out of advanced materials sewn into vests and other clothing. It is much more comfortable than wearing heavy metal plates. The most famous material used in soft body armor is Kevlar.

KEVLAR

Like Nomex, Kevlar is another amazing synthetic material found in the real world. Lightweight and flexible, Kevlar is about five times stronger than steel. Its stretching strength is eight times greater than steel wire.

Kevlar is strong due to its chemical structure. Its long molecule chains are naturally arranged in regular parallel lines, like spaghetti in a package. But the chains also form bonds between each other, as if you've glued all the spaghetti together. This makes the material extraordinarily tough.

Inside police vests are many layers of tightly woven Kevlar.

Kevlar is often made into fibers that are knitted very tightly together. Tight knitting makes the material even stronger. Kevlar is so strong, it's used in automobile brake pads and chain saw-proof clothing. Kevlar is even used to strengthen aircraft bodies and ropes that anchor battleships.

Kevlar can be woven and used to protect any part of the body. In fact, Nomex and Kevlar can be blended together to protect against fire, cuts, and impacts. Firefighter gear is often made of a Nomex and Kevlar mix. But the most well-known use of Kevlar is in bulletproof vests.

FACT:

STEPHANIE KWOLEK, A CHEMIST AT DUPONT, INVENTED KEVLAR IN 1964.

CERAMIC PLATES

STRIKE FACE

ceramic plate

Sometimes soldiers or police need more than Kevlar protection. For that they turn to hard body armor. This armor is often made of steel or ceramic plates.

Steel is very durable and less expensive, but it is heavy to wear. Ceramic plates are used to make light armor that offers excellent protection. These plates are as strong as steel but 70 percent lighter. Ceramic plates can be made of various materials. Some of the strongest are made of a powder called boron carbide. This powder is pressed and heated to about 4,000°F (2,204°C). After baking, the plates are nearly as hard as diamond.

Ceramic plates will still shatter on impact, but that's not a bad thing. Shattering the plate spreads out and reduces the energy of a bullet or blow.

A DIFFICULT CHOICE

In real life, soldiers and police have to compromise between safety and mobility. To move easily, they can wear less or lighter armor. But that means their level of protection decreases. If they wear heavier armor with more protection, they weigh themselves down. Heavier armor makes it harder for officers to move or respond quickly. For police and soldiers in the line of fire, it's a difficult choice to make.

dier puts on a body armor vest
e a mission in Afghanistan.

Brawling with archenemies can be tough on any crime fighter's hands and feet. That's why gloves and boots are key parts of Batman's suit. But these common pieces of clothing hide more science than meets the eye.

GLOVES AND GAUNTLETS

The long gloves Batman wears are called gauntlets. They give his hands and arms much needed protection from punches, kicks, and weapons.

Originally, a gauntlet was a glove worn with plate or chain mail. It was lined with leather and covered in metal. It protected the hands and forearms from blows. Chain mail may no longer be in style, but protective gloves and gauntlets haven't gone away.

gauntlets

All sorts of people from lumberjacks to chefs use gloves and gauntlets. They protect workers from assembly-line blades, knives, sheet metal, and chain saws. Chemists use gauntlets to protect their forearms and hands from dangerous chemical spills. Shoulder-length Kevlar gauntlets help protect the arms of soldiers from flying metal and other dangers.

Many athletes also wear protective gauntlets as part of their uniforms. Kendo and fencing both require gloves and gauntlets. In kendo, long thickly padded fabric and leather gloves called *kote* protect the forearms, wrists, and hands. Fencers wear lightly padded gloves that may be made of leather or of washable materials.

Welders wear thick gauntlets to protect their hands from burns.

BOOTS AND BATS

In more ways than one, Batman is a well-heeled super hero. His rugged boots protect his feet as he scales Gotham City's skyscrapers. But it's the sonic device he sometimes carries in his heel that will make your jaw drop. This device creates a high-frequency sound that only bats can hear. With a push of a button, Batman can call bats to create a diversion.

Real-world scientists don't have sonic devices to call bats. But they do use loudspeakers, microphones, and special electronic "ears" to study the sounds bats make. Bats send out high-frequency sound waves that bounce off objects in their paths. People can't hear these sounds, but bats can. They listen to the echoes of these sounds to locate nearby objects. Their incredible power is known as echolocation.

Insect-eating bats use echolocation to find food. They keep track of the time between making a sound and hearing its echo return. A bat's echolocation system is very precise. Scientists study it in hopes of making radar and sonar equipment even better.

FACT:
IN 1940 SCIENTIST DONALD GRIFFIN DISCOVERED BATS USE SOUND TO FIND THEIR WAY IN THE DARK. HE COINED THE WORD "ECHOLOCATION" TO DESCRIBE WHAT THEY DO.

SOUND WEAPONS

Calling for some bat backup isn't the only use for the Caped Crusader's sonic device. It can also bring his foes to their knees by giving them terrible headaches.

Using sound as a weapon isn't limited to science fiction. High-intensity sounds really can cause headaches, ringing of the ears, and permanent hearing loss. Although they have limited use, sonic weapons actually exist.

Police and the military have used Long Range Acoustic Devices (LRADs) to break up crowds during protests and riots. These "sound cannons" can broadcast messages and shrill tones at least 1,600 feet (488 meters). On full power an LRAD can emit a concentrated sound of about 150 decibels. This sound equals hearing a gunshot less than 3 feet (.9 m) away. The LRAD can also focus sound in a narrow "beam," allowing it to be aimed at a specific target. In 2005 the cruise ship *Seabourn Spirit* used an LRAD against pirates off the coast of Somalia.

A sailor aims an LRAD at a small craft approaching the USS *Blue Ridge*.

THE MOSQUITO

Younger people can hear higher-pitched noises better than older people. This fact inspired Howard Stapleton of Wales to create a sonic device he named the Mosquito. The device makes an extremely annoying high-pitched noise that only young people can hear. Thousands of the devices have been sold since its invention in 2005. Parks, cities, and schools use the Mosquito to help drive away loitering teenagers.

To hide his identity, Batman wears a cowl. This hooded mask disguises his features and makes him look threatening. But the cowl does a lot more than look cool. It protects his head from impacts. It also has a bunch of amazing devices built in.

HEAD PROTECTION

In the real world, protecting your head is serious business. A helmet's job is to protect against head and brain injuries. To do that, helmets are made of different materials depending on their use. For example, military helmets often have Kevlar to protect against bullets and shrapnel.

While they're made for different uses, most helmets have a similar construction. They often have a soft inner foam liner to absorb an impact's energy. They also have a hard outer shell that spreads an impact's force over a larger area. Some shells are made of tough plastic. But many are made of composite materials. Composite materials are lightweight, very strong, and easy to shape. They are made by binding one material with the fibers or fragments of a stronger material. Fiberglass, developed in the 1930s, was one of the first modern composites. It's made up of very fine glass threads and plastic to hold the glass fibers together. Carbon-fiber composites are even stronger. They are made of carbon fibers and a hardened resin, such as epoxy.

A pit crew member wears a helmet to protect against accidents during a race.

LIGHTER, STRONGER, FASTER

Carbon-fiber composite materials combine high strength with low weight. As a result, they are used extensively in Formula One race cars. Most commonly, the car's frame and running gear are made from these materials. The lighter the race car, the faster it can go.

LONG-DISTANCE HEARING

One key to fighting crime is to figure out what criminals are up to. To do this, the "ears" of Batman's cowl carry microphones. These microphones send audio to a sound amplifier. Batman can hear anything he's pointed at, even if he's not near the target.

A parabolic microphone picks up the sounds of the game from the sidelines.

In the real world, long-distance eavesdropping is done with parabolic microphones. These listening devices use a bowl-shaped reflector to collect and focus sound waves onto a receiver. They collect sound waves the same way a satellite dish collects radio waves. Such microphones pick up sounds from 300 yards (274 m) away. People use parabolic microphones to record sounds from nature and to collect audio from football sidelines. They are also used in police surveillance and for spying.

People can also listen in on conversations using tiny devices called bugs. Bugs are hidden microphones that secretly pick up sounds and send them to transmitters or receivers. Bugs can be disguised as batteries or appliance plugs. They can be as small as pencil erasers, making them easy to hide in walls or furniture.

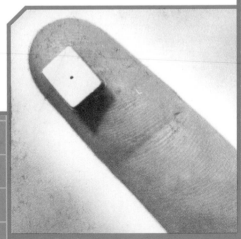
Bugs use miniature microphones that are smaller than a fingertip.

SEEING IN THE DARK

Just like a bat, Batman is most active at night. But even the Dark Knight needs help peering through the gloom. To boost his eyesight, Batman's cowl often includes night-vision lenses. These high-tech specs help him see in the dark.

Seeing in the dark starts with the science of light. Light energy travels in waves of different lengths. The light we can see is called visible light. But some light waves are too short or too long for us to see. The shorter waves include gamma rays, X-rays, and ultraviolet rays. The longer waves include infrared light, microwaves, and radio waves.

Thermal imaging shows hot water running from a faucet.

One method to see in the dark uses infrared light instead of visible light. Infrared light waves carry heat. All objects give off infrared light waves. Thermal imaging picks up these waves and changes them into visible light. Thermal night-vision goggles let you see people, animals, and objects by the heat patterns they give off. They don't need any visible light at all.

FACT:

FIREFIGHTERS USE THERMAL IMAGING TO SEE THROUGH SMOKE. THEY FIND PEOPLE BY THE BODY HEAT THEY GIVE OFF.

ENHANCING THE IMAGE

Thermal imaging isn't the only way people see in the dark. Most night-vision gear uses image enhancement. This technology creates the eerie, glowing green night-vision images people see in movies.

Image enhancement collects any available light and makes the most of it. Even in the dimmest conditions, all objects reflect some light. Night-vision goggles with image enhancement use an image-intensifier tube. It gathers and boosts available light to make objects look brighter. Unfortunately, some of the detail and all of the color is lost during the enhancement process.

So why do objects seen with image enhancement look green instead of black and white? Night-vision goggles produce green pictures because human eyes are most sensitive to green light. The human eye can make out more shades of green than any other color.

THERMAL OR ENHANCED?

Which night-vision technology is better? That depends on what you're looking for. Thermal imaging can be used day or night in smoke, fog, and dust storms. But the equipment is more expensive, larger, and heavier. Image enhancement only works in the dark, but it is cheaper and the images are also easier to make out. But camouflage can still trick image enhancement technology. Thermal imaging, however, can find hidden objects by the heat they give off.

A soldier tests the settings on a night-vision scope.

We've all seen Batman perched atop one of Gotham City's skyscrapers. His watchful eye scans the city. His cape flaps in the wind. But Batman's cape doesn't only make him look like an awesome super hero. It also helps him glide safely through the air.

GLIDING THROUGH GOTHAM CITY

Batman's ability to glide is similar to how hang gliders work. A hang glider is basically a curved triangle-shaped wing. The wing lets air flow over its surface to make it rise. Hang glider pilots rise into the air by taking off from mountaintops, cliffs, or other high spots. The movement of air over the surface of the wing generates lift, the force that counters gravity. This force keeps the glider aloft.

Powered aircraft require a motor, propeller, or jet engines to stay up in the air. Hang gliders need air movement. If the air is still, the glider will fall at a rate of roughly 200 feet (61 m) per minute. To stay aloft, a glider pilot needs to find and use thermals. These columns of warm air occur when the sun heats the air and causes it to rise. A pilot catches a thermal by circling the warm air, which pushes him or her upward. Strong thermals can lift a hang glider thousands of feet in minutes!

DISTANCE CHAMP

Hang glider pilots can easily fly 100 miles (161 kilometers) in a single flight. But Dustin Martin did better than that. In 2012 he set the world record for distance by traveling 474 miles (763 km) from Zapata to Lorenzo, Texas. The flight took just more than 11 hours.

WINGSUIT FLYING

Batman's cape makes gliding to the ground look easy. In real life, gliding is a little trickier—and more dangerous. But it's not impossible. Some thrill seekers wear wingsuits to jump from extreme heights and glide through the air.

Wingsuits have webbed wing surfaces between the legs and under the arms. During a jump, the air inflates these surfaces by passing through inlets in the suit. The suit becomes a giant wing. It makes the wingsuiter look like a huge flying squirrel.

Wingsuiters deal with the same forces of flight that planes and hang gliders do. When a wingsuiter jumps out of a plane, gravity pulls him or her down. The average skydiver falls to Earth at a rate of 120 miles (193 km) per hour. Wingsuits cut that speed by more than half. Wingsuiters can land safely because they use parachutes to slow themselves down before reaching the ground.

A wingsuiter glides through the air above Tianmen Mountain in China.

GARY CONNERY

In 2012 a British daredevil named Gary Connery completed a 2,400-foot (732-m) wingsuit dive from a helicopter. He dived into an area stacked with nearly 19,000 cardboard boxes to help cushion his fall. Connery became the first person in the world to jump out of an aircraft and land safely without using a parachute.

BATARANGS
AND
GRAPNELS

THE SCIENCE BEHIND
BATMAN'S UTILITY BELT

BATARANGS AND GRAPNEL GUNS

The Batarangs and grapnel gun on Batman's Utility Belt would make any super hero jealous. But you don't have to be a super hero to find their connections to the real world.

BOOMERANG BASICS

When Batman has a criminal on the run, he often reaches for his Batarangs. The Caped Crusader has used these bat-shaped weapons throughout his career. While Batman has several types of Batarangs, some of them work like boomerangs.

Most people picture a boomerang as a curved stick that returns after being thrown. But not all boomerangs come back. In fact, many ancient boomerangs were hunting weapons that didn't return. They were shaped throwing sticks that flew well through the air.

Boomerangs that can return to the thrower are different. They usually have two wings joined in the middle. Set at a slight tilt, these wings allow air to flow over their surfaces. This airflow creates lift.

When thrown, a returning boomerang has two kinds of motion—a spinning motion and a forward motion. The spinning motion causes uneven lift on the wings. One wing moves forward in the direction of the flight. The other wing moves backward against the direction of the flight.

While uneven lift tries to tip the boomerang over, the spinning motion twists the tipping forces at right angles. Together these forces give the boomerang its curved flight. It's similar to how leaning on a moving bike makes it turn. Thrown correctly, a boomerang's circular flight brings it back to the thrower.

A boomerang is held correctly when its curve points toward the thrower.

FACT:

SOME BOOMERANGS CAN HAVE THREE OR EVEN FOUR WINGS. MORE WINGS ALLOW THE BOOMERANG TO TURN IN TIGHTER CIRCLES.

STEALTHY SHURIKEN

Sometimes Batman uses Batarangs to smash windows, take out lights, and create distractions. In these cases, his Batarangs act more like Japanese throwing weapons called *shuriken*.

Shuriken date back hundreds of years to the time of samurai and ninja. These Japanese warriors were famous for their swords and fearsome fighting skills. But shuriken made excellent backup weapons. The shuriken's shallow points often weren't deadly. But they could easily catch an enemy off guard when thrown at their hands, feet, or face.

In the United States, shuriken are called throwing stars and ninja stars. But don't let these names fool you. Shuriken can have many different shapes. Historically, there were two basic designs: *bo shuriken* and *hira shuriken*.

Bo shuriken were straight, spikelike blades. They were often called "throwing needles." They had either one or two pointed ends. They worked like darts or arrows. Bo shuriken were thrown overhand like a baseball pitch.

Hira shuriken are more familiar to most people. These thin, star-shaped metal plates had sharpened blade tips. Unlike bo shuriken, hira shuriken had three to eight razor-sharp points. With a sharp flick of the wrist, hira shuriken were sent spinning through the air.

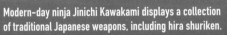

Modern-day ninja Jinichi Kawakami displays a collection
of traditional Japanese weapons, including hira shuriken.

45

GRIPPING GRAPNELS

Sometimes Batman needs to rise above the concrete canyons of Gotham City. In these situations he fires his grapnel, or grappling hook, device. With a pull of the trigger, his grapnel and line help him scale skyscrapers.

The Romans invented grappling hooks more than 2,000 years ago. In naval battles, they threw dozens of grappling hooks to snag enemy ships. Then they'd pull the ships close enough for their soldiers to board.

Devices for firing grappling hooks exist today. But they're not nearly as small as Batman's. Digital Force Technologies has developed a tactical pneumatic launch system (T-PLS) for the U.S. Army. This system uses compressed air. It launches a titanium grappling hook and a Kevlar line 120 feet (37 m) in the air.

But don't plan on adding a T-PLS to your own Utility Belt anytime soon. This launcher weighs 19 pounds (8.6 kilograms). It measures about 4 feet (1.2 m) long.

The T-PLS also doesn't have a winch to pull you up the side of a building. You have to climb the rope yourself. Even so, the T-PLS is a handy military tool.

A soldier practices throwing a grappling hook during training.

ATLAS POWER ASCENDER

In 2005 a group of students at the Massachusetts Institute of Technology created a battery-powered rope ascender. The lightweight device, called the Atlas Power Ascender, is about the size of a power tool. It pulls a fully-geared soldier or firefighter up a rope at about 10 feet (3 m) per second.

AMAZING ROPE

Without a second thought, Batman leaps off Gotham City's tallest skyscrapers. As he plunges toward the ground, the line from his grapnel holds firm. He gracefully swoops down on his enemies. To survive these falls, Batman's lines have the strength of climbing ropes and the flexibility of bungee cords.

Climbers use static ropes to rappel down mountains.

In real life, ropes are designed to handle the different stresses people put on them. Mountaineers and rock climbers use dynamic ropes. These ropes stretch like elastic. Stretching helps them absorb some of the energy if a climber falls. If the rope didn't stretch, the jolt from a 20-foot (6-m) free fall could break a climber's back.

Hauling equipment and rappelling require rope that doesn't stretch. In these situations, people use static ropes instead. Static ropes are very durable, but they aren't designed to stop free falls. They provide safety for people working in high places, for rescue work, for caving, and other similar activities.

Bungee jumpers use cords made up of strands of elastic material such as natural rubber. These strands are wrapped in a tough outer cover made of cotton or nylon. Bungee cords extend and regain their shape easily. They can stretch three to four times their original length before springing back.

An assistant holds the bungee cord of a bungee jumper preparing to leap off a cliff.

FACT:

SOME STATIC ROPES ARE MADE FROM KEVLAR, THE SAME MATERIAL USED IN BULLETPROOF VESTS. KEVLAR ROPES ARE SO STRONG THAT THEY'RE USED IN DEEP SEA AND OUTER SPACE EXPLORATION.

Batman doesn't just fight crime—he stops it cold. With bolas, blowguns, and a tamper-proof Utility Belt, he stays one step ahead of his enemies.

THE BUSINESS OF BOLAS

If Batarangs don't knock villains off their feet, Batman's bolas trip them up. A bola is a throwing weapon made of weights connected with cords. Just like boomerangs, bolas were used as weapons and for hunting. They helped catch animals and birds by entangling their legs or wings. If thrown with enough force, bolas could even break bones.

Ancient hunters used bolas as effective weapons for catching prey.

Bolas date back thousands of years to the Stone Age. Over the centuries, the Inuit and the Chinese used them for hunting and warfare. South American gauchos, or cowboys, also used them to capture cattle by snaring their legs.

The bolas gauchos used had braided leather cords. The weights were usually wooden balls or small leather sacks filled with stones. Some bolas were works of art. They were made of ivory and covered with valuable metals.

Bolas had different names based on the number of weights. A *perdida* had one weight. A *boleadora* had three. Perdidas were usually used against people. Boleadoras were used for hunting wild cattle and large birds. Some bolas had up to eight weights.

BACKYARD BOLAS

Does anyone still use bolas today? Look no further than a game known as ladder ball, ladder toss, or lasso golf. This modern lawn game uses bolas. The game is played by throwing a two-ball bola onto a plastic ladder. Each ladder rung has a point value. The game's goal is to wrap the bolas around the rungs to score the most points.

OUT FOR THE COUNT

Batman doesn't use guns—at least not ones that fire bullets. But he does have weapons to disable his enemies. For a quick knockout punch, he relies on his blowgun and tranquilizer darts.

In real life, tranquilizer darts aren't used on people. Instead, they're used for capturing wild animals. The darts are commonly fired from a tranquilizer gun or rifle. These weapons usually get their power from compressed gas cartridges. The burst of gas sends the tranquilizer-filled dart flying at the target.

The tranquilizers used in darts can be sedative, anesthetic, or paralytic drugs. Sedatives relax and calm an animal. Anesthetics knock them out. Paralytic drugs paralyze an animal's muscles so it can't move.

The drug dose needed to tranquilize an animal is based on its estimated weight. Heavier animals need a larger dose than smaller ones. But weight isn't the only deciding factor. Slowing down an excited elephant takes twice the dose as a calm elephant. And whenever an animal is darted, an antidote must be on hand. This drug reverses the tranquilizer's effect.

A veterinarian holds a tranquilizer dart used to sedate an elephant.

STUNNING SCIENCE

The amazing gadgets on Batman's Utility Belt get the most attention. But there's more to the belt itself than meets the eye. It is armed to stop criminals from tampering with it. These defenses don't cause permanent harm. But they do keep the Utility Belt from falling into the wrong hands.

Real-life duty belts aren't armed to stop people from taking them. But they do carry nonlethal weapons, such as Tasers, for controlling attackers. Tasers are electronic devices that can target someone from 20 feet (6 m) away. They allow officers to keep a safe distance while controlling a suspect.

A police officer carries a yellow Taser on his duty belt.

How does a Taser work? When the device is fired, two metal darts, or probes, fly at the target. The probes attach to the target and remain connected to the device with thin copper wires. Once the probes attach, they send electric pulses between each other. These pulses disrupt nerve communication between the muscles and the brain. The shock temporarily paralyzes the muscles. Most targets drop straight to the ground.

THE BODY ELECTRIC

Electronic control devices upset your body's electrical communication system. That's right, your body is electric! In fact, everything you do is controlled by electrical signals. Your body parts use small doses of electricity to communicate with each other. The electricity travels along your nerves and between your brain cells.

FACT:

A TASER'S PROBES DON'T NEED TO TOUCH SKIN. THEY'LL WORK EVEN IF THEY'RE SNAGGED IN CLOTHING.

AN EXPLOSIVE ARSENAL

Sometimes Batman needs something with a bit more bang than a Batarang can deliver. From smoke bombs to flashbangs, the Caped Crusader has a variety of explosives. They help him control angry mobs, crash criminal hideouts, or make quick getaways.

DISAPPEARING ACT

Batman's skills make him a master of surprise. He often slips in and out of areas undetected. But even the Dark Knight sometimes needs help getting out of tight spots. Luckily, his Utility Belt carries smoke bombs to cover his escapes.

Smoke bombs are a type of firework. Instead of exploding with a shower of light, they produce huge clouds of smoke.

Many smoke bombs are walnut-sized hollow clay or cardboard balls filled with smoke-making chemicals. Some smoke bombs are lit directly. Others have a time-delayed ignition that uses a short fuse.

Either way, lighting the materials inside a smoke bomb causes a chemical reaction. The reaction produces gases and particles that combine to create a thick cloud of smoke. A typical smoke bomb releases smoke for about 10 to 15 seconds—just long enough to make a quick getaway.

Smoke bombs come in different sizes and shapes and can release all sorts of colors.

IGNITION ON IMPACT!

Batman's smoke bombs are sometimes ignited by impact rather than by lighting a fuse. In this case, the ignition source is a material used in Christmas crackers and bang snaps. The material is responsible for the loud "crack" you hear.

SMOKE SCREEN

Batman uses smoke to help create distractions. In the real world, militaries use smoke screens in sea and land warfare for the same reason. They cause panic, confusion, and low visibility.

The ancient Greeks used smoke screens during the Peloponnesian War (431–404 BC). They even burned wood soaked with pitch and sulfur to create toxic arsenic smoke. Smoke screens also played a role in World War II (1939–1945). Huge smoke generators created screens that were miles long to help hide troop movements.

Today modern armies use smoke grenades. These small canister-type grenades work as signaling devices, landing-zone markers, and smoke screens. Instead of being lit, they are activated by removing a pin.

Military smoke grenades don't just release white smoke. Soldiers have all the colors of the rainbow at their fingertips. Red, orange, green, blue, violet, black, gray, and white all have their uses. The range of colors helps soldiers in aircraft spot different things happening on the ground. For example, red smoke might signal a bombing target or green smoke a wounded soldier.

Soldiers use a yellow smoke screen to mask their movements.

FACT:

PAINTBALL WARRIORS USE SMOKE GRENADES TO COVER THEIR MOVEMENTS FROM OPPONENTS.

FLASH AND BANG

Sometimes Batman needs more than just smoke to distract his enemies. In these instances, he reaches for his flash grenades. Flash grenades are also known as stun grenades and flashbangs.

Flashbangs are nonlethal explosives that confuse an enemy's senses. When detonated, a chemical reaction creates a blinding flash of light. This extremely bright flash makes it impossible to see for about five seconds.

A soldier throws a flashbang during a training exercise.

At the same time, the detonation also creates a loud bang of about 160 decibels. That's louder than standing next to a jet taking off. This earsplitting noise causes short-term hearing loss. The blast even disturbs the fluid in the inner ear, making enemies lose their sense of balance.

Soldiers and police officers use flashbangs during drug raids or hostage situations. They have also been used to storm hijacked airliners and break up prison riots. Flashbangs give officers a few seconds to secure any threats.

FACT:

DECIBELS ARE USED TO MEASURE SOUND INTENSITY. NORMAL BREATHING IS ABOUT 10 DECIBELS. A RUNNING VACUUM CLEANER IS ABOUT 70 DECIBELS. A JET ENGINE TAKING OFF IS 130 DECIBELS.

MAKING THE BAD GUYS CRY

Batman doesn't back down from a fight. But sometimes there are just too many foes for even a super hero to handle. If the Caped Crusader runs out of smoke bombs and flash grenades, he clears the way with tear gas pellets.

Soldiers and police officers use tear gas to help control unruly crowds and rioters. It is often released with canisters or grenades. The canisters can be thrown by hand or launched with mortars and riot guns.

National Guard soldiers practice using tear gas during training exercises.

The chemicals in tear gas are irritants. They create a burning sensation in the eyes, nose, mouth, and lungs. They cause coughing, choking, and crying. The good news is that the symptoms usually go away within an hour.

Tear gas isn't the only irritant that police officers use. They can also subdue people with pepper spray. This spray is made from hot chili peppers. It causes a burning sensation on any exposed skin, as well as crying, coughing, and difficulty breathing.

FEELING THE BURN

The military and police departments have policies for using pepper spray. As part of their training, they usually expose themselves to the spray. Doing this allows them to experience the effects of pepper spray before using it on someone else.

BOMBS AWAY

Besides smoke bombs, Batman carries a variety of explosives on his Utility Belt. He uses them to blow up locks, destroy weapons, or disable villains' getaway cars. Many of his explosives are small bombs known as mini-grenades.

Grenades have been used in warfare for hundreds of years. Early grenades were just metal containers filled with gunpowder. Soldiers lit the wick and tossed the grenade before it could blow up in their hands.

Modern time-delayed grenades are far more sophisticated. The outer shell of the grenade is made of cast iron. It holds a chemical fuse, which is surrounded by explosive material. A spring-loaded striker triggers the grenade's firing mechanism. The striker is held in place by the striker lever. This lever is held in place by the safety pin.

Soldiers in the 12th Combat Aviation Brigade practice throwing hand grenades.

pin →

To ignite the grenade, the soldier pulls out the pin and throws the grenade. Once thrown, the spring-loaded striker hits a percussion cap. This impact creates a spark that lights the fuse. The fuse takes about four seconds to burn. When the fuse burns down to the detonator, the grenade explodes.

KA-BOOM!

Lobbing grenades works in some situations, but others require a more direct punch. Villains rarely leave the doors to their hideouts unlocked. To bust into their lairs, Batman uses powerful explosives.

Explosives are chemicals that, once ignited, undergo a very fast chemical reaction. The reaction releases gases that expand very rapidly and become very hot.

In real life explosives are often used for demolition. But they're also used in construction for building roads, dams, and railroads, and excavating foundations and tunnels.

Artists have used explosives to blast out huge monuments from mountains, such as the Crazy Horse Memorial and Mount Rushmore in South Dakota. Dynamite helped carve out 90 percent of Mount Rushmore.

Explosives are also used in extracting metals, rock, and minerals from the ground. Millions of tons of explosives are used in the United States each year. In fact, most of the explosives used in the U.S. are for mining coal.

The military uses explosives to destroy a weapons stockpile in Baghdad, Iraq.

The military also uses explosives. Soldiers use special plastic explosives to demolish large obstacles and heavy walls. Plastic explosives combine explosive chemicals with a plastic binder material. This mixture makes the explosive material moldable and putty-like. It also makes the explosive safer to handle.

FACT:

SWEDISH CHEMIST ALFRED NOBEL, THE FOUNDER OF THE NOBEL PRIZE, IS CONSIDERED THE FATHER OF EXPLOSIVES. HE INVENTED DYNAMITE IN THE 1860S. HE ALSO INVENTED GELIGNITE, THE FIRST PLASTIC EXPLOSIVE.

PREPARED FOR ANYTHING

Batman must always be ready for anything—from studying crime scenes to traveling underwater. Luckily, his Utility Belt is loaded with more than just weapons. It always has the right tools for any task.

WATCHFUL EYES

Batman does much of his detective work from the shadows. He keeps a watchful eye on criminals without being seen himself. One tool that helps him see around and over walls is a periscope.

Periscopes use two mirrors to reflect light around corners. Light coming into the periscope bounces off a mirror set at a 45-degree angle. The reflected light travels down the periscope to a second mirror. This mirror sends the light to the user's eye.

Periscopes are very important for the military. Armored M1 Abrams tanks use periscopes to see the battlefield. Without leaving the tank, a commander uses several periscopes to see the entire surrounding area. Submarines also use periscopes. Sailors can see what's going on above the waves, even when the sub floats below them. In fact, a sub's periscope can be up to 60 feet (18 m) long.

A Marine using a hand-held periscope.

PHOTONICS MASTS

Periscopes on submarines may soon be a thing of the past. Photonics masts are replacing periscopes. They have digital equipment and sensors. A photonics mast rises above the water in a way similar to a car antenna. It holds infrared sensors and digital cameras. Images appear on display panels inside the sub.

FACT:

THE LONGER THE TUBE IN A PERISCOPE, THE SMALLER THE IMAGE LOOKS. PERISCOPES IN TANKS AND SUBMARINES HAVE MAGNIFYING LENSES BETWEEN THE MIRRORS. THEY MAKE THE REFLECTED IMAGE LARGER.

CHECKING FOR PRINTS

As a superb detective, Batman has a keen eye for evidence villains leave behind. As a result, one of his most useful gadgets is his portable fingerprint analysis kit. It allows him to inspect fingerprints left at the scene of a crime.

Everyone has a unique pattern of ridges, valleys, and whorls on his or her fingertips. Police detectives study these patterns. If a person's fingerprints match those found at a crime scene, he or she could be a suspect.

For fingerprint identification, detectives look for visible and latent fingerprints. Visible prints are made on a surface that can hold an impression. Dirt and clay, for example, can sometimes hold prints that detectives can see.

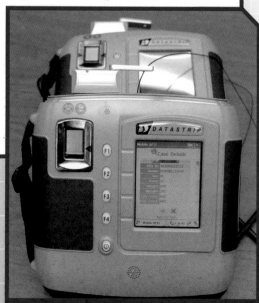

Portable Automated Fingerprint Identification Systems allow police officers to compare fingerprints at a crime scene with the fingerprints of known criminals.

Latent fingerprints can't be seen with the naked eye. They're made when sweat and oil on the skin leave prints on doorknobs, windows, or weapons. Investigators find latent prints by dusting surfaces with fine powders. Then they use lasers and other light sources to spot where the powders stick to prints. Investigators "lift" these prints with tape or take photos of them.

Police departments have access to the stored fingerprints of millions of known criminals. Computer programs help compare the fresh prints with fingerprints in a database. When they find a match, detectives are one step closer to catching the criminal.

UNDERWATER DANGERS

Aquaman can breathe in the ocean's depths, but Batman needs a little help. For missions that take the Caped Crusader underwater, the rebreather on his Utility Belt helps him survive.

Advanced scuba divers and U.S. Navy SEALs also use rebreathers. These devices allow divers to breathe their own air over and over again. A chemical scrubber in the device removes carbon dioxide gas breathed out by the diver. Leftover oxygen and other gases are breathed in again.

Rebreathing air has its limits. As needed, the device also injects fresh oxygen from a small oxygen tank. It also controls the amount of oxygen being breathed in. Too much or too little oxygen can be dangerous.

A military diver uses a rebreather to move through the water.

Though expensive, rebreathers have some advantages over regular scuba equipment. They don't waste oxygen because they replace only what is used up. They also weigh less than normal scuba gear. Most importantly, rebreathers don't create bubbles. For military uses, rebreathers won't give away a diver's position to the enemy.

scuba gear

rebreather

A diver using a rebreather doesn't release air bubbles like a diver using scuba gear.

BATMOBILES AND BATCYCLES

THE ENGINEERING BEHIND BATMAN'S VEHICLES

PERFORMANCE STANDARDS

Batman depends on his road vehicles. Powerful engines and precise steering ensure that no enemy is a match for the Batmobile or the Batcycle. But Batman's advanced technologies are not all super hero fiction.

POWER BOOSTS

Chasing down Gotham City's super-villains requires maximum power from Batman's vehicles. To achieve it, he experiments with a variety of high-tech engines. These engines include turbochargers and atomic energy. In the real world, airplanes have used turbocharged engines since the early 1900s. These engines increase power. They pump an extra dose of an air-gas mixture into the engine's cylinders. The extra air-gas produces more power when burned. Turbocharged engines boost the power of regular engines by 30 to 40 percent.

turbocharger

The 1962 Oldsmobile Jetfire was one of the first cars to use a turbocharger. But early turbocharged car engines were unreliable. Carmakers stopped making them until high gas prices and better engineering brought them back. Today turbocharging gives small cars more power and better gas mileage.

The BMW 328i sedan is one of many modern cars that boasts a turbocharged engine.

ATOMIC ENERGY

Turbochargers are cool, but what about atomic engines? In 1954 the USS *Nautilus* became the first submarine to use an atomic engine. This engine allowed the sub to stay underwater longer than any previous submarine. In 1958 the *Nautilus* became the first known vessel to reach the North Pole. It traveled under the arctic ice to get there.

RAPID ACCELERATION

Flame-releasing power bursts are signature moves of the Batmobile and the Batcycle. Rocket thrusters give Batman fast starts and rapid acceleration. They always leave the bad guys eating dust.

Normal cars don't have rocket thrusters, but some experimental cars do. One such vehicle is the British rocket-propelled Thrust Supersonic Car (SSC). It was built with two 20,000-pound (9,100-kilogram) Rolls-Royce Spey engines. These huge engines were originally designed for jet planes.

Swansea University
Prifysgol Abertawe

EPSRC serco UWE BRISTOL STP

element Protocol

ROYAL AIR FORCE

On October 15, 1997, ThrustSSC proved just how fast it could go. British fighter pilot Andy Green tested the car in

the Black Rock Desert in Nevada. He reached 763 miles (1,228 km) per hour. ThrustSSC set the world record as the fastest land vehicle on Earth. It also became the first car to break the speed of sound.

ThrustSSC

FACT:

ENGINEER JAMES WATTS (1736–1819) COINED THE TERM HORSEPOWER. IT MEASURES AN ENGINE'S POWER BY COMPARING IT TO THE AMOUNT OF WORK A DRAFT HORSE CAN DO.

BLOODHOUND SSC

Bloodhound SSC is another British built rocket car. It is designed to go even faster than ThrustSSC. It hopes to use a jet engine to reach about 230 miles (370 km) per hour. Then it will fire a rocket to reach more than 1,000 miles (1,600 km) per hour. At full speed, the engine will run at about 80,000 horsepower. That's equal to the power of 95 Formula One race cars.

HAMPSON

Bloodhound SSC

TIGHT CORNERING

In car chases, taking corners with speed is key. To keep Batman in the hunt, the Batmobile and Batcycle sometimes use unique axle and wheel designs. These features help his vehicles make extremely tight corners and 360-degree turns.

To find innovative cornering systems in the real world, look no further than Bimota in Italy. The motorcycle company's Tesi 3D uses hub-centered steering. This motorcycle looks different because it doesn't have a fork connected to its front wheel. Instead, horizontal bars extend from the side of the bike. These bars push and pull the wheel when the handlebars turn. This mechanism allows the wheel to rotate more freely on its axle. The Tesi 3D gives riders quicker, steadier turns than traditional motorcycles.

The Tesi 3D doesn't have a traditional fork connected to the front wheel.

The Airtrax Sidewinder 3000's angled rollers make tight turns.

Motorcycles aren't the only cool rides with unique wheels. The wheels on the Airtrax Sidewinder 3000 will make you do a double take. This omnidirectional forklift uses a circular set of angled rollers as wheels. When in motion, these rollers act like a ball. They allow the forklift to move in any direction—even sideways. In packed warehouses the Sidewinder easily glides through tight spaces.

STEER-BY-WIRE HANDLING

Racing through the streets of Gotham City puts a high demand on the Batmobile's steering system. Luckily, Batman doesn't have to rely on traditional mechanical steering. Computers and sensors help the Batmobile make hairpin turns.

Engineers usually design cars with a system of rods and gears that connect the steering wheel to the front tires. Turning the steering wheel physically turns the tires too. But steer-by-wire technology breaks from tradition. It controls steering without a mechanical link between the steering wheel and the front tires.

Instead of rods and gears, steer-by-wire uses computer sensors and wires. It sends movements from the steering wheel to computer sensors. The sensors then send the information to electric motors that move the tires. Engineers believe that steer-by-wire may someday allow people to control cars with keyboards, joysticks, or even body movements.

In 2013 Nissan unveiled the first major production car with steer-by-wire technology. The Infiniti Q50 uses sensors to send the driver's steering movements to the wheels. Infiniti has a back-up system that reconnects the steering wheel to the wheels in cases of electrical failure.

Infiniti Q50

FLY BY WIRE

Airliners have used fly-by-wire technology for decades. In 1972 a Navy F-8 Crusader became the first airplane to test it. Since then

most aircraft use fly-by-wire technology for safer flights. Fly-by-wire allows signals from a computer to make adjustments on wing and tail flaps. These signals replace mechanical pulleys, cranks, and cables a pilot would otherwise need to operate.

You've experienced the brawn of the Batmobile and Batcycle. But their smart technologies really set them apart from other vehicles. With stealth mode, ejection seats, and other capabilities, there's almost nothing these vehicles can't do.

STEALTH MODE

The chase is on. But with enemies on its tail, the Batmobile suddenly disappears. Where did it go? With its lights off and a quiet engine, the Batmobile has entered stealth mode.

The F-22 Raptor's body shape and covering help it stay hidden from enemy radar.

Hiding in plain sight has been a military goal for decades. Although complete invisibility isn't possible, some aircraft can disappear from enemy radar. Radar systems send out bursts of radio energy. When it hits an object, the energy bounces back and shows the object's location. Absorbing or deflecting radar signals hides an object's location.

In the 1980s the U.S. military unveiled the first stealth aircraft. The F-117A fighter jet's sharp edges and angles reflected radar at odd angles. Its surface was also coated with a top-secret radar absorbent material (RAM). These technologies made the plane look like a small bird on radar screens. The military retired the F-117A in 2008, but other stealth aircraft have taken its place. These stealth flyers include the B-2 Spirit, F-22 Raptor, and F-35 Lightning.

TOO STEALTHY?

Stealth mode has its drawbacks. Electric and hybrid car engines make almost no noise. Their silence is dangerous for bikers and walkers who don't hear them coming. In 2013 the U.S. National Highway Traffic Safety Administration (NHTSA) proposed a new rule. It would require that these vehicles add noisemakers to their engines.

SELF-DESTRUCT CAPABILITY

Both the Batmobile and the Batcycle would be dangerous weapons in the wrong hands. Luckily, Batman can always use his self-destruct mechanisms as a last resort. He can blow up his vehicles to protect their secret technology.

Self-destructing electronics have the ability to dissolve in water.

These days, secret electronic systems are packed into almost every military vehicle and weapon. Keeping these systems out of enemy hands is a huge concern. But in real life, self-destruction doesn't always mean a fiery explosion.

The U.S. Defense Department's Defense Advanced Research Projects Agency (DARPA) works on self-destruct technology. Its Vanishing Programmable Resources (VAPR) program has even developed electronics that dissolve in water. These devices are now being studied for use in self-dissolving biomedical implants. These medical sensors could dissolve instead of requiring surgery for removal.

But DARPA wants to take self-destructing technology to the battlefield as well. The agency is seeking ways to make reliable electronics that work only as long as they are needed. They also hope to design devices that use a remote control to dissolve on command.

SHUTTLE SELF-DESTRUCT

The first two minutes of a NASA space launch are critical. If a spacecraft veers off course, populated areas could be in danger. For this reason, NASA's space shuttles were equipped to self-destruct. During launches, an Air Force officer sat at a flight termination panel. If the shuttle ever malfunctioned, the officer needed to flip two switches. These switches would arm and detonate explosives on the shuttle's rocket boosters.

EJECTION SEAT

The Batmobile crashes through the guardrail and careens off the edge of a bridge. The vehicle plunges toward the river below. Is it game over for Batman? Not likely. The Batmobile's ejection seat ensures his survival.

Ejection seats are a common real-world technology in aircraft. They have been standard equipment in most military aircraft since World War II. These days ejection seats are one of the most complicated systems on an aircraft. They have thousands of parts. Each part must work flawlessly to save a pilot's life.

An Air Force pilot ejects from a fighter jet after guiding it safely away from an air show crowd.

The entire ejection sequence happens in just four action-packed seconds. In an emergency a pilot pulls a handle. Explosive bolts then blast off the cockpit canopy. A rocket motor launches the seat up to 200 feet (61 m) above the plane. When the pilot is safely away from the plane, a small parachute opens. As the pilot falls, a sensor tracks his or her altitude. When a safe altitude is reached, the main parachute opens. At the same time, a motor blasts the ejection seat away from the pilot. The pilot then floats to the ground.

ACES II

U.S. Air Force planes use Advanced Concept Ejection Seats (ACES II). These "smart seats" decide when to release parachutes. They also sense when the seat is tumbling out of control. The seats use small rockets to counteract the tumbling forces.

FACT:

EJECTION SEATS HAVE BEEN SUCCESSFULLY USED IN AIRCRAFT FLYING AT SPEEDS UP TO 800 MILES (1,287 KM) PER HOUR.

SHAPE-SHIFTING

There's no trapping the Batmobile or the Batcycle. Just when they appear cornered, these vehicles drop large parts to squeak through narrow alleys. This ability to change shape allows Batman's vehicles to escape dangerous situations.

Shape-shifting technology isn't pure science fiction. Engineers are developing amazing vehicles and robots that shape shift. In Germany, BMW has produced the GINA Light Visionary Model. This sporty concept car doesn't have a metal body. Instead, GINA covers a skeletal aluminum frame with a stretchy fabric. The touch of a button alters the shape of the frame. Then the fabric expands or contracts to the new shape. GINA isn't for sale, but can be seen at the BMW museum in Munich, Germany.

DARPA has also developed a shape-shifting material called programmable matter. This matter is composed of flexible electronics that can be programmed to shift into different shapes. So far DARPA's research has produced a tiny paper-thin robot. Like origami the robot folds itself into a boat or airplane shape. Then it unfolds and flattens itself. This technology could lead to more advanced robots that squeak through tiny cracks to perform missions.

BMW's GINA has a fabric body that stretches and contracts as the car's skeletal frame changes shape.

FACT:

A CONCEPT CAR IS PRODUCED TO SHOWCASE A NEW STYLE OR TECHNOLOGY. IT IS TESTED AND SHOWN TO THE PUBLIC FOR REACTIONS BEFORE IT IS PRODUCED FOR SALE.

MULTI-FUNCTION

It's a car. It's a plane. It's a boat. No, it's all three! Batman's vehicles are way more than what they seem. They can easily change function to perform where the action takes them.

Vehicles that can transition between environments have been around for ages. An amphibious tug called the Alligator helped loggers haul cargo over land and water in the 1880s. In 1937 the Waterman Aerobile took to the skies as the first flying car. But time-consuming transitions made these early vehicles impractical.

Modern vehicles perform quick changes when they transition. The Gibbs Humdinga changes from land vehicle to watercraft in as little as five seconds. Its **suspension** uses sensors to detect when water is deep enough to float. Then the Humdinga's wheels and brakes fold up into its body. A supercharged V-8 engine powers the vehicle on land. Twin jets push it through the water. It can travel more than 30 miles (48 km) per hour on water. It reaches highway speeds on land.

The wheels of a Gibbs Humdinga peek out of the water as it glides across a marina.

Going from land to water is one thing. But what about leaving the open road for the clear blue sky? The Terrafugia Transition is a car with folding wings. On land it drives like a regular car and fits in a garage. To take flight, the Terrafugia unfolds its wings and cruises at about 105 miles (169 km) per hour. It can fly up to 490 miles (789 km) on a single tank of gas.

The Terrafugia Transition's folding wings allow it to drive down the road like a car.

JUMP CAPABILITIES

Crumbling bridges and gaping gulches are no match for the Batmobile or Batcycle. These incredible vehicles can hurtle between building tops across Gotham City's skyline. Can real vehicles do that too?

Jumping cars and motorcycles in the real world usually involves a ramp. A ramp helps the vehicle gain enough upward thrust to counteract gravity. But the vehicle's take-off angle determines its landing angle. Without a landing ramp, the front of the car or bike will crumple on impact. Even with the ramp, the vehicle takes quite a jolt. Therefore, engineers design special suspension systems to ensure safe landings.

How far can a real car jump? Travis Pastrana found out on December 31, 2009. He launched off a ramp at about 100 miles (161 km) per hour. He cleared a distance of 269 feet (82 m). It was the world's longest jump with a car.

Travis Pastrana flies through the air during his record-breaking jump in 2009.

SANDFLEA

A small robotic car designed by Boston Dynamics is capable of jumping without a ramp. The SandFlea can jump up to 30 feet (9 m) in the air. It is powered by a carbon dioxide charged piston. The SandFlea weighs only 11 pounds (5 kg). The U.S. Army is testing the SandFlea for use in future missions.

SUPERSTRONG AND SECURE

Few vehicles have safety features that match the Batmobile's or Batcycle's. No disaster or explosion slows these vehicles down. Their armored bodies and bulletproof tires keep them rolling.

BULLETPROOF AND EXPLOSION-PROOF BODIES

The Batmobile is one of the toughest cars ever designed. It deflects bullets. It blasts through walls of flames. But are real-world vehicles able to handle these conditions?

Armored trucks and military vehicles use bulletproof and explosion-proof technology. They are outfitted with ceramic plates, Kevlar fabric, and bulletproof glass.

A soldier peers through the bulletproof glass of a heavily armored Humvee gun turret.

The ceramic plates in armored trucks and military Humvees aren't made out of the same ceramic as coffee mugs. These slabs of baked boron carbide are so hard they're sometimes called "black diamond." Bullets shatter when they hit these slabs. Ceramic plates are often layered with reinforced plastics or fabrics. They are placed inside door panels or attached to the outside skin of military vehicles.

Kevlar fabric is also used for bulletproofing. This tightly woven fabric is similar to nylon but stronger. It is almost impossible to tear or melt. Layers of Kevlar absorb a bullet's energy to slow it down and stop it.

Windows present a unique bulletproofing challenge. Bulletproof windows are made of a polycarbonate layer sandwiched between regular glass. Polycarbonate is a tough plastic. A bullet breaks through the layers of regular glass, but is stopped by the polycarbonate layer.

THE BEAST

The U.S. president's limo may be the only car that compares to the Batmobile for its armor. The president's limousine is nicknamed "The Beast." On top of body armor, it is decked out with night-vision cameras and Kevlar tires. For extra protection, the limo has its own oxygen supply. It also has a backup blood supply for the president.

BULLETPROOF TIRES

Dodging enemy fire and off-road driving take a toll on ordinary tires. But Batman doesn't have time for a flat. Whether using puncture-proof or auxiliary tires, Batman's vehicles get him to his destination every time.

In the real world, you might be riding on a set of high-tech tires without ever knowing it. Military vehicles and some passenger cars use run-flat tires. Normal tires need to be filled with air, like a balloon. The air pressure inside the tire holds up the weight of the car. When these tires puncture, they lose air and can't be driven. Run-flat tires have stiff sidewalls to support the weight of the car. Even without air, a run-flat tire can be driven up to 100 miles (161 km).

Auxiliary supported tires are another type of high-tech tire. They are built like a tire inside a tire. Their solid inner ring carries the weight of the vehicle if the outer tire blows out. Michelin's PAX auxiliary tire can run flat for up to 125 miles (200 km) at 55 miles (89 km) per hour.

inner ring

The solid inner ring supports an auxiliary tire in the event of a flat.

HONEYCOMB TIRES

The U.S. military asked engineers to come up with a tire design that doesn't use air at all. Resilient Technologies and the University of Wisconsin–Madison answered this engineering challenge. They designed a tire polymer constructed in a honeycombed pattern. This tire can withstand an explosion and still make a speedy getaway.

Batman's vehicles are all about attitude. They talk to Batman and drive themselves. And don't even think about hiding from the Batmobile or the Batcycle. They sense everything around them.

REMOTE DRIVE

The Batmobile's self-driving feature is a super hero's dream. Batman can call his car with a remote control. It then winds its way through Gotham City for a speedy pickup.

In the real world, Google has been testing self-driving cars since 2010. A Google car charts a course toward a programmed location. It heads out using cameras and a fast-spinning laser eye. These tools see traffic lights, stop signs, and other cars on the road. The car's computers react to this information. Google cars have logged more than 300,000 miles (483,000 km) of driving with no reported accidents.

Totally driverless cars are years away, but some cars already help with simple driving tasks. BMW's traffic jam assistant helps control the car in stop-and-go traffic jams. As long as the driver keeps one hand on the wheel, the car stays a constant distance from the vehicle ahead of it. The car also keeps itself in its own lane.

The sensor on the roof of a Google car helps it navigate the streets of Washington, D.C.

SPIRIT OF BERLIN

Spirit of Berlin is a car controlled by a cell phone app. Students at a university in Berlin, Germany, developed the app to control the car's steering, braking, and acceleration. A camera placed on the car's dashboard sends video to a smartphone user. The user drives the car using the phone's touch screen.

VOICE ACTIVATION AND RECOGNITION

Batman's vehicles are more than just tools. They are allies in the fight against the forces of evil. Not only does Batman talk to his vehicles, but they listen and talk back.

Voice activation and recognition are a reality in some of today's vehicles. General Motors uses Apple's Siri technology in some of its cars. With Siri, drivers simply speak and their cars obey. A car using Siri changes music and locates restaurants or shops through voice activation. It can even check schedules and make appointments. What if Siri doesn't understand your command? Then it asks you questions to clarify.

Ford's SYNC technology recognizes and responds to the driver's voice. SYNC can tell the difference between a driver's voice and loud traffic or the radio. It learns how a driver says certain words and responds to his or her accent. With simple voice commands, SYNC helps drivers make phone calls, control music, and get traffic directions.

An attendee at a technology show tries a demonstration on a SYNC control console.

ENGAGING THE ENEMY

Batman's vehicles excel at tracking down notorious criminals and detecting their weapons. The Batmobile and Batcycle help foil evil schemes and defend justice at every turn. Luckily, the real world has many of Batman's defensive technologies.

WEAPONS DETECTION SYSTEM

The villains of Gotham City will stop at nothing to rid themselves of the Caped Crusader. And they have a stash of high-powered weapons to get the job done. But the Batmobile's weapons detection system is always on alert for potential threats.

Weapons detection is a huge concern at airports around the world. Since 2006 Advanced Imaging Technology (AIT) has helped look for hidden weapons. These machines use microwaves to scan a person's body. They create an image of a person's body and locate any suspicious objects. These scanners are more sensitive than older metal detectors. They not only find metal weapons, but also plastic explosives and ceramic knives.

An airline passenger raises her arms as she is scanned by an AIT machine.

The military has special detectors to track and identify chemical and biological weapons. These detectors are called Biological Integrated Detection Systems (BIDS). BIDS mount to Humvees or Black Hawk helicopters. They use lasers to scan the air and detect unnatural agents. These systems quickly find chemical and biological weapons and alert soldiers to the danger.

The Ohio National Guard shows off a BIDS mounted on the top of a Humvee.

FAST M²

Since 2008 the Department of Homeland Security has been testing a new way to find people planning to commit crimes. The Future Attribute Screening Technology Mobile Module (FAST M²) scans eye movements, heart rates, gestures, and facial expressions. Rapid heart rates and eye movements could mean a person is up to no good.

WEAPONS

When it comes to weapons, Batman's vehicles have more under the hood than just raw firepower. In road battles, Batman always aims to disable his enemies. To accomplish this, his vehicles often use disruptive weapons such as caltrops and smoke screens.

Caltrops have been around for thousands of years. These spiky weapons made effective low-tech land mines for ancient and medieval warriors. Scattering them on roadways and across the countryside slowed down advancing armies. Caltrops injured horses and camels, and they tripped up foot soldiers.

Military and police forces still use caltrops in the form of spike strips. Spike strips are rows of metal spikes. They are laid out on a road in front of a speeding car. They puncture tires and disable getaway vehicles.

A soldier puts down a spike strip at a checkpoint in Iraq.

Smoke screens also have modern uses. Soldiers use smoke screens to hide their movements from the enemy. Some banks also use smoke screens to prevent burglaries. When robbers enter a vault, the touch of a button causes thick smoke to suddenly fill the air. When the robbers lose their bearings, they usually take off or get caught.

Soldiers crouch behind a smoke screen to conceal their movements.

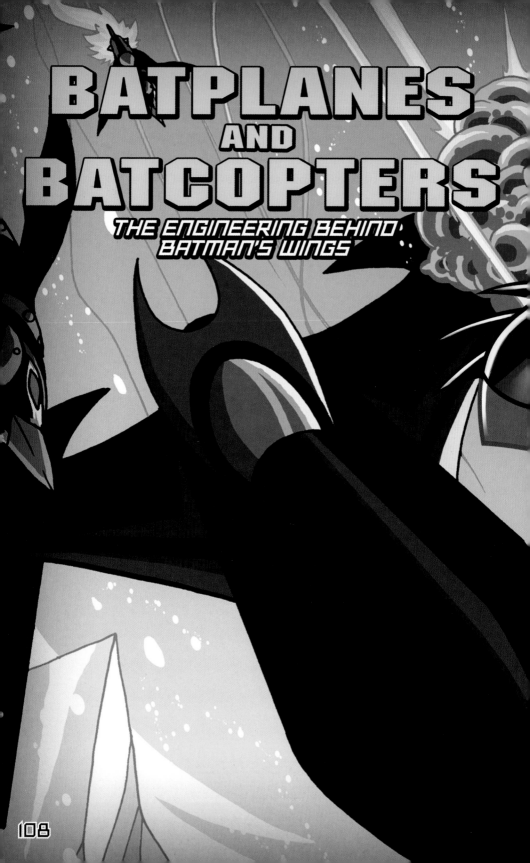

BATPLANES AND BATCOPTERS

THE ENGINEERING BEHIND BATMAN'S WINGS

Batplanes and Batcopters seem to fly like no other aircraft. With sleek shapes, jet-powered engines, and spinning blades they handle the harshest conditions.

AERODYNAMICS

There's no mistaking the Batplane. Its black body and wings make it look like a bat in flight. But is its design for looks or for function? The answer is a little of both.

Most real aircraft look similar to animals in flight. In particular, airplanes look like soaring birds or flying bats—and for good reason. Early studies in aerodynamics were based on bird flight. In the 1890s German engineer Otto Lilienthal built gliders by studying bird wings. Aircraft today still use his designs for wing shapes.

Otto Lilienthal tests one of his gliders in 1895.

Modern airplane wings are rounded on the front and tapered toward the back. As an airplane moves, this shape allows air to flow faster over the top of the wings. At the same time, air moves slower under the wings. The unequal pressure pushes the plane upward. This pressure is called lift. A pilot changes the amount of lift by adjusting flaps on the wings. These flaps also allow the airplane to turn and slow down for landings.

SMART BIRD

Airplane wings can't flap like a bird's wings. But engineers at the German company Festo are changing that. They have designed the Smart Bird. This robotic bird has a 6.5-foot (2-m) wingspan. It flaps its wings like a seagull. The Smart Bird may one day lead to new engineering designs for manned aircraft.

SUPERSONIC JETS

When enemy missiles lock onto the Batplane, the Dark Knight needs all the speed he can get. Luckily, jet engines power his aircraft. Not only does he outrun enemy fire, but he also shatters the speed of sound.

Jet powered aircraft got their start in 1939. The first jet plane was a German designed Heinkel He 178. Its top speed was 373 miles (600 km) per hour. Since then, all jet engines use the same basic idea. Their power comes from injecting and burning fuel in an engine chamber. As the fuel burns, rapidly

Heinkel He 178

expanding gases burst from the engine. These gases create the thrust that pushes the plane forward.

Some modern jets travel so fast they break the speed of sound. But traveling faster than 768 miles (1,236 km) per hour has a drawback. It creates an earsplitting sonic boom. A sonic boom happens when a jet suddenly shoves air molecules out of its way. The shock waves that result sound like loud thunder. The larger the plane and the closer it flies to the ground, the louder the boom. A boom can be so loud that it can hurt people's eardrums or damage buildings.

An F-18 Super Hornet creates a vapor cone as it breaks the speed of sound.

LYNX SPACECRAFT

XCOR Aerospace has a new plan for supersonic flight. Its *Lynx* spacecraft will take off from a runway much like a normal plane. Rocket engines will lift the spacecraft almost straight up. They will take the *Lynx* outside Earth's atmosphere for short space flights. Then the spacecraft will glide back down to the runway. For $100,000 space tourists can already start booking future *Lynx* flights.

FACT:

NASA'S X-43A SET THE WORLD RECORD AS THE FASTEST AIRCRAFT ON NOVEMBER 16, 2004. IT REACHED A SPEED OF NEARLY 7,000 MILES (11,265 KM) PER HOUR.

ROTOR POWER

Speed and power can only get Batman so far in the Batplane. To move around in tight areas, he needs the rotor power of the Batcopter. Rotors allow this whirlybird to sneak between skyscrapers or land on a busy street.

In the real world, helicopters use rotors to lift off and land in places airplanes can't. The science behind a helicopter's rotors is the key to its flight. A helicopter has two sets of rotors. The main rotor on top has large blades that slice through the air. They create lift that allows the helicopter to rise. The smaller rotor on the helicopter's tail balances out the main rotor. Without the tail rotor, a helicopter would spin out of control.

Spinning rotors allow an MH-60S Seahawk helicopter to hover above a ship's deck.

Helicopters don't need runways for takeoffs. But they work a lot harder than airplanes do to stay in the air. Helicopters use a lot more fuel and travel slower than airplanes. Most helicopters fly at speeds between 100 to 200 miles (161 to 322 km) per hour.

EUROCOPTER X3

The Eurocopter X3 uses a unique rotor design. This experimental helicopter has rotors on its sides. These rotors help keep the helicopter stable. They also allow it to gain more speed than a regular helicopter. The X3 reaches speeds of about 270 miles (435 km) per hour.

EXTRA ORDINARY PROPULSION

Batplanes and Batcopters buzz around like planes and helicopters. But sometimes their propulsion systems seem out of this world. Where are their propellers? Where are their jets? What's powering these aircraft?

Jets and traditional rotors are not the only ways to propel aircraft. Real-world engineers are working on new forms of propulsion. The Moller International's Skycar 400 uses ducted fans for vertical takeoffs and flight. Skycar 400 is a prototype vehicle currently running flight tests. Its designers hope this personal aircraft will someday replace cars.

Moller International's Skycar 400 hovers in the air during a test flight.

The D-Dalus uses four barrel-shaped spinning rotors to rise into the air and stay aloft.

Austrian Innovative Aeronautical Technology has developed yet another type of propulsion system. The D-Dalus was first shown at the 2011 Paris Airshow. It is neither a helicopter nor a fixed winged aircraft. The D-Dalus' four rotors spin in different ways and face opposite directions. The unmanned craft can launch vertically, rotate, and hover without traditional rotors or wings. It can lift up to 150 lbs (68 kg).

Flying above Gotham City's streets is more dangerous than driving on them. Batman must weave between skyscrapers and hover in midair. Fortunately, the Batplane and Batcopter are up to the task.

SHORT TAKEOFFS AND LANDINGS

The Batplane has touched down on a busy city street. But with no runway, there's no way the aircraft can take off. Or is there? The Batplane suddenly lifts itself into the sky. Who needs long runways with the ability to take off from tight spaces?

In the real world, most airplanes need about 2,300 feet (700 m) of runway to take off and land. But fighter jets on aircraft carriers only use about 300 feet (90 m). How can they use such short runways?

For most fighter jets, catapults and tail hooks are the key. For takeoffs, the jet's front wheels hook to a catapult cable. The pilot revs the plane's engines to full throttle. Then a high-pressure piston pulls the plane down the runway. It flings the jet off the aircraft carrier. The plane reaches 170 miles (274 km) per hour in just two seconds!

An F-18 Super Hornet traps an arresting cable as it lands on the deck of an aircraft carrier.

Landing on an aircraft carrier is one of the riskiest tasks for a fighter jet pilot. The pilot must use the jet's tail hook to trap an arresting cable stretched across the ship's deck. In the landing approach, the pilot pushes the jet to full power. If the tail hook misses the cable, the pilot heads back into the air. If the tail hook traps the cable, the jet slows down rapidly.

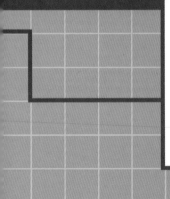

FACT:

LAUNCHING AIRCRAFT OFF SHIPS DATES BACK TO WORLD WAR I (1914–1918). THE NAVY CATAPULTED ITS FIRST AIRCRAFT OFF THE USS *NORTH CAROLINA* ON NOVEMBER 5, 1915.

GOING VERTICAL

Short takeoffs and landings are amazing. But what if you have no runway at all? The Batplane's vertical takeoffs and landings seem impossible for a plane. But the Ryan X-13 Vertijet and the Harrier Jump Jet prove otherwise.

The tail-sitting Ryan X-13 Vertijet mastered vertical takeoffs and landings more the 50 years ago. This small jet was called a tail-sitter. It took off and landed on its tail. The plane was designed to launch from a submarine. The Vertijet made history on April 11, 1957. A pilot launched it

A Ryan X-13 Vertijet comes in for a landing.

like a rocket, but flew it like a plane. Then he landed the Vertijet back on its tail. Because the Vertijet was difficult to land, only two prototypes were built and tested. But the plane paved the way for the Harrier Jump Jet.

The Harrier Jump Jet first took to the skies in the late 1960s. Its thrusters direct power from the jet engines downward. This downward thrust allows the Harrier to make completely vertical takeoffs and landings. Once airborne, the pilot changes the thrusters' angle and power for normal flight.

The Harrier combines the best of helicopter and fighter jet technology. It not only takes off and lands in tight spaces, but also reaches speeds of 730 miles (1,175 km) per hour. That's almost four times faster than a traditional helicopter.

A night-vision camera captures the vertical thrust of the Harrier Jump Jet as it lands.

HOVERING

Batman hovers over Gotham City in the Batcopter. With such convenient midair parking, keeping an eye out for criminal activity is a cinch. But how do real helicopters manage to stay in place high in the air?

We've all seen helicopters hover above the ground. This ability is important in rescue missions and when loading and unloading cargo.

Hovering in midair isn't easy. Gravity always pulls the helicopter toward the ground. In addition, wind gusts push the helicopter around. To stay in one spot, pilots constantly adjust the rotor controls to balance these forces.

With all of these forces acting on a helicopter, is it possible to hover without a pilot? On May 22, 2012, U.S. marines completed the first "hot hook up" using a K-MAX unmanned helicopter. As the unpiloted helicopter hovered overhead, marines attached cargo to a cable hanging from the craft. Unlike other unmanned air vehicles, K-MAXs aren't flown remotely by a pilot on the ground. They fly almost completely by themselves based on programmed instructions.

A K-MAX unmanned helicopter prepares for takeoff in Afghanistan.

LASER HOVERING

LaserMotive, a Seattle-based company, has developed a small model helicopter that hovers with the help of a laser beam. From the ground, the laser is aimed at power cells under the helicopter. The power cells change the laser light into electricity. With this power, the rotors keep the mini aircraft hovering in the air.

In Batman's quest for justice, he disables enemies with a variety of weapons. The Batcopter's whirling vortex stomps out riots. The Batplane's guided missiles disable targets with precision.

VORTEX WEAPONS

Gotham City's police force is no match for a raging mob. But Batman has things under control. He uses the Batcopter's vortex to control the situation. This swirling downdraft from the rotors forces rioters to the ground.

The military and police forces work on developing nonlethal weapons that disable targets. In fact, the U.S. military developed and studied a vortex ring gun for crowd control in 1998. This weapon sent out a high-speed ring of air.

Researchers test the strength of a vortex ring gun for the military.

The ring was powerful enough to knock down a 150-pound (68-kg) mannequin 30 feet (9 m) away. The military also studied adding pepper spray to the shock wave to strengthen its punch. While the vortex ring gun worked, it wasn't precise enough for real-world use.

The military may have shelved its device, but vortex technology is used to solve other real life problems. A hail cannon blasts storm clouds with shock waves to prevent hailstones from forming. Why prevent hailstones? Millions of dollars worth of crops are destroyed each year by hail. Explosive gases inside a hail cannon fire 200-mile (322-km) per hour shock waves into thunderstorms. These waves seek to break up hail before it hits tender crops and fragile greenhouses. But do hail cannons really work? Scientists have their doubts, but many farmers believe they do.

A hail canon stands ready to protect a vineyard from hail.

PRECISION MISSILES

As a defender of justice, Batman protects the lives of innocent people and criminals alike. His goal is always to disarm his enemies. To do that, the missiles on his aircraft are very precise. They only seek out and lock onto the targets Batman wants to strike.

Precision guided missiles are called smart bombs. They are programmed or steered toward their target. Modern smart bombs include Television/Infrared (TV/IR) bombs, laser-guided missiles, Joint Direct Attack Munitions (JDAM), and heat-seeking missiles.

A TV/IR bomb has a TV or an infrared camera mounted to its nose. The camera sends video to a controller. The controller uses the video to steer the bomb toward its target.

A sailor performs final maintenance on a JDAM bomb prior to a flight mission.

Laser-guided missiles use laser-seeking devices. These devices hunt for lasers being "painted" on targets. When a seeker finds a laser, a missile locks onto the target and explodes on impact.

JDAMs are guidance kits. They change regular bombs into smart bombs. JDAM bombs are each programmed with the GPS coordinates for their targets. Up to 80 JDAMs can drop from a plane in one pass. Each one can seek out a different target.

Heat-seeking missiles are used for air-to-air combat. A heat-seeker senses the heat from an enemy aircraft. It guides itself toward this heat source before exploding.

FACT:

THE SIDEWINDER HEAT-SEEKING MISSILE IS 9 FEET, 5 INCHES (2.9 M) LONG. IT WEIGHS 188 POUNDS (85 KG). IT CAN TRAVEL MORE THAN 10 MILES (16 KM) TO ITS TARGET. EACH SIDEWINDER COSTS ABOUT $84,000.

STEALTH MODE

Batplanes and Batcopters give the Dark Knight the element of surprise. They help him hide from enemies and mount sneak attacks. When Batman's aircraft operate in stealth mode, they can't be seen or heard. More importantly, they can't be detected by radar.

Radar is a burst of radio energy that scans an air space. When it hits an object, the energy bounces back. This "echo" shows the location of the object. To sneak up on an enemy, aircraft must avoid radar detection.

The B-2 Spirit is a U.S. military fighter jet. This stealth plane has a flat shape and sharp angles for a reason. Its shape allows radar to pass by it or to be reflected off it at odd angles. The B-2 also has noise shields on its engines. It can fly very close to an enemy before its powerful engines are heard.

The B-2 Spirit's flat shape and sharp angles allow it to hide from enemy radar.

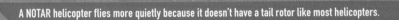

A NOTAR helicopter flies more quietly because it doesn't have a tail rotor like most helicopters.

Helicopters fly lower than planes, so they can usually hide from radar detection. But their rotors make a lot of noise. Reducing rotor noise is the key to making a helicopter stealthy. Some stealth designs try to reduce noise by enclosing the tail rotor. Others change the angles of the main rotors. McDonnell-Douglas' NOTAR helicopter uses no tail rotor at all. A jet of air provides thrust to overcome the twisting forces of the main rotor.

The Batplane and Batcopter have a mix of tricks to help the Dark Knight do his job. From airlifts to ejection systems, Batman's aircraft have solutions for nearly every situation.

SKYHOOK

When Batman gets backed into a corner, the only way out is up. In these situations his air vehicles come to the rescue. In mid-flight, they use ladders and cables to pluck the Caped Crusader right off the ground.

Rescue workers use helicopters to airlift injured climbers off mountains every year. But what about being lifted off the ground by a plane flying at 125 miles (200 km) per hour? It sounds like science fiction, but it's not. In the 1960s the Central Intelligence Agency (CIA) began using Skyhook. This system allowed a low-flying plane to pluck people off the ground without ever landing.

A Navy sailor is lifted out of the water during testing of the Skyhook system.

To perform a Skyhook rescue, a packet was airdropped to a person on the ground. Inside were a harness, a high-strength nylon rope, and a weather balloon. The person on the ground hooked himself into the harness. The balloon was inflated using a portable helium bottle. The balloon pulled the 500-foot (152-m) rope into the air. Then a passing plane snagged the rope with forks attached to its nose. After releasing the weather balloon, the passenger was reeled onboard the back of the plane with a winch.

Illustrated instructions showed soldiers how to use Skyhook safely.

OPERATION COLDFEET

In 1962 Operation Coldfeet became the first official mission to use Skyhook. The CIA successfully pulled two people from the arctic ice. They had been exploring an abandoned Soviet Union ice station.

EJECTION SYSTEM

The Batplane just took a hit. It's spiraling out of the sky. Is this the end of the line for the Dark Knight? No way. Batman's ejection system propels him to safety.

Many military aircraft have ejection systems. When activated, an aircraft's system blasts the top off the cockpit. A rocket motor launches the seat into the air to get the pilot safely away from the plane. Sensors track his or her altitude, opening parachutes and releasing the seat at a safe height. If landing over water, a survival kit drops down with a self-inflating life jacket and raft attached.

Some aircraft fly so high they need escape pods to help pilots survive in the thin, cold air. One of the first aircraft escape pods was installed in the B-58 Hustler in the 1960s. The pods could eject a flight crew traveling twice the speed of sound at 70,000 feet (21,000 m) above Earth. They sealed each crew member into clamlike capsules with their own oxygen. Parachutes released to help the pods land safely. If they landed in water, the clamshells opened to become floating rafts.

The B-58 Hustler's escape pods sealed crew members up in clamlike capsules.

SPACE ESCAPE POD

Escape pods are very important for space travel. Astronauts wouldn't survive a disaster without a navigable escape pod. The *International Space Station* always has a Russian-built *Soyuz* escape pod ready for speedy escapes. This three-person pod can support life for up to three days.

The top of a *Soyuz* rocket holds the escape pod used on the *International Space Station*.

CHANGING SHAPE

Every good crime fighter must adapt to changing situations. Nowhere is that more true than with Batman's aircraft. Whether it's lengthening a wing or folding the Batplane into a boat, shape-shifting comes in handy.

Modern planes can't morph as much as the Batplane. But real-world engineers are experimenting with wings and blades that twist and change shape. Even small changes in wing shape can improve control or reduce aircraft noise.

NASA has developed and tested a warping airplane wing called an active aeroelastic wing (AAW). A Boeing F/A-18 was fitted with AAWs for test flights in 2002. Tabs and slats on the wings twisted to make the plane bank and roll with less drag. Future AAW technology could result in 10 to 20 percent lighter wings, making flight more efficient.

Want a quieter, smoother helicopter ride? NASA is also experimenting with shape-changing helicopter blades. The key to the blades are piezoelectric materials. These "smart materials" flex and morph when an electric shock is sent through them. Testing has shown that controlling blade shape can cut a helicopter's noise in half.

Active aeroelastic wings allowed NASA's F/A-18 to maneuver in the air with less drag.

THE WRIGHT BROTHERS

Orville and Wilber Wright were warping the wings of their aircraft long before NASA. In 1903 the Wright brothers' first aircraft didn't have the wing flaps of modern planes. Cables connected the wing tips to the pilot's saddle. The movement of the pilot's hips warped the wings and turned the plane.

UNMANNED FLIGHT

Batman often has his hands full. It's not always possible for him to get to his aircraft when he needs it. Sometimes it needs to come to him. In these situations, his high-tech autopilot enables the Batplane to fly as an unmanned aircraft.

Unmanned flight is a booming area of engineering and technology. The U.S. military has more than 10,000 unmanned aircraft. These drones perform both spy and attack missions.

An Air Force MQ-9 Reaper comes in for a landing in Afghanistan.

The Raven is the world's most used spy drone. It weighs only 4.2 pounds (1.9 kg). It's small enough to fit in a backpack. Once tossed into the air, the Raven flies for up to 80 minutes. It zips along at 30 miles (48 km) per hour. It sends video or infrared images back to a pilot up to 9 miles (14 km) away. Troops use the Raven to peer over mountaintops to search for enemies.

The MQ-9 Reaper is the world's most advanced combat drone. It has been flying missions in Afghanistan since 2007. From 50,000 feet (15,240 m) above Earth, Reaper locates, locks on, and follows moving targets. Its cameras record suspicious activity and its guided missiles take out targets. Reaper travels 230 miles (370 km) per hour. It is controlled from miles away using satellite technology.

NANO HUMMINGBIRD

One of the newest spy drones is the size of a humming bird. AeroVironment developed this mini drone at a cost of $4 million. Nano Hummigbird can fly up to 11 miles (18 km) per hour. It flies through open windows and perches on wires. Its tiny camera spies on anything it flies over.

Batman's aircraft take the Caped Crusader where few others can go. To do that, they sometimes use the best of both airplane and helicopter technology.

HELICOPTER AND AIRPLANE

Is it a helicopter? Is it an airplane? Sometimes Batman's aircraft act like both. They take off and land like helicopters. But they also fly fast like jets. Does the real world have anything similar?

The U.S. military began developing aircraft that could work like a helicopter and an airplane in the 1950s. These efforts paid off when the Bell Boeing V-22 Osprey took flight in 1989. It was the world's first tilt-rotor.

The Osprey is called a tilt-rotor because its rotors tilt. Tilting rotors allow it to change from helicopter-mode to airplane-mode in mid-flight. When the Osprey's rotors swing vertically, the aircraft flies like a helicopter. When the rotors turn horizontally, they become airplane propellers. The Osprey changes from helicopter to airplane in as little as 12 seconds.

The Osprey travels twice as fast as a typical helicopter. It can carry up to 20,000 pounds (9,072 kg) of cargo or 24 soldiers. It is easily stored on aircraft carriers. Its rotors fold up and its wings rotate. The military uses the Osprey for assault and rescue missions.

Two Osprey prepare to take off vertically from the deck of a ship.

AUTOGYRO

Every so often Batman flies an aircraft so strange you'd think it must be pure fiction. For instance, in early adventures Batman buzzed around in a one-man Bat-Gyro. But what was this strange vehicle and is it real?

Autogyros, also called gyroplanes, are neither science fiction nor old-fashioned. These lightweight vehicles look like helicopters. They can even perform many of the same tasks as helicopters. But they fly more like airplanes.

Spanish engineer Juan de la Cierva invented the autogyro in 1920. Later helicopter designs used Cierva's ideas. An autogyro's engine and its smaller propeller push it through the air. Unlike a helicopter, an engine doesn't power its main rotor. This rotor is angled to catch air currents and provide lift.

Juan de la Cierva stands with one of his early autogyros.

Autogyros are efficient and low cost. Police officers and soldiers use them for rescue missions. They also can carry mobile medical labs. Autogyros can even be fitted with skis or floats to land on snow or water.

A modern two-person autogyro soars high above the ground.

Batman's gear has changed dramatically over the years. His Batsuit and Utility Belt may have begun as parts of a simple disguise, but they have evolved into technological marvels. Likewise, his Batmobile and Batplane have also transformed into high-tech tools for battling the forces of evil. But Batman's amazing technology is more than just a product of an imaginary world. It's a stunning reflection of the science and engineering all around us.

Just as Batman battles the forces of evil, scientists and engineers tackle the challenges of our world. They develop products like Kevlar and Nomex to protect against firefights and flames. They work with the military to develop stealth vehicles that slip through enemy lines. They even help us soar through the air with hang gliders and wingsuits. In thousands of ways, scientists and engineers remind us that fact is as amazing as fiction.

Best of all, Batman's connections to our world inspire us to look to the future. What kind of gear will the Caped Crusader develop in the years to come? No one knows for sure. But keep an eye on real-world advancements in science and technology. They'll likely show up in Batman's adventures.

INDEX